SNAKES FOR KIDS

SNAKES FOR KIDS

A JUNIOR SCIENTIST'S GUIDE to Venom, Scales, and Life in the Wild

JUNIOR SCIENTISTS

MICHAEL G. STARKEY

ROCKRIDGE PRESS

To my son, Noah, and every other child with a curiosity about nature:

May you always have the opportunity to explore our extraordinary world and learn about its unique and fascinating wildlife.

For general information on our other products and services or to obtain technical support, please contact our Customer Care Department within the United States at (866) 744-2665, or outside the United States at (510) 253-0500.

Rockridge Press publishes its books in a variety of electronic and print formats. Some content that appears in print may not be available in electronic books, and vice versa.

Interior and Cover Designer: Emma Hall
Art Producer: Tom Hood
Senior Editor: Sabrina Young
Associate Editor: Maxine Marshall
Production Editor: Emily Sheehan

Illustrations @ Kate Francis, 2020. Photographs: Sebastian Kennerknecht / Minden Pictures, cover; Dorling Kindersley Ltd/Alamy, pp. ii, 26, 28, 35, 45; Life on White/Alamy, pp. vi, vii, 18, 19, 27, 46, 59, 60, 62; Matthijs Kuijpers/Alamy, pp. viii, 1, 23, 25, 34, 38, 53, 54, 58; Joseph T. Collins/Science Source, p. 20; Larry Miller/Science Source, p. 21; Chris Mattison/FLPA/Science Source, p. 22; dwi putra/Alamy, p. 24; A.B. Sheldon/Dembinsky Photo Associates/Alamy, p. 29; John Cancalosi/Alamy, p. 30; John Serrao//Science Source, p. 31; Andrew DuBois/Alamy, p. 33; Buiten-Beeld/Alamy, p. 37; petographer/Alamy, p. 39; GH Photos/Alamy, p. 40; Petlin Dmitry/Alamy, p. 41; Roberto Nistri/Alamy, p. 42; John Sullivan/Alamy, p. 43; David Chapman/Alamy, p. 44; blickwinkel/Alamy, pp. 48, 49; Ken Griffiths/Alamy, p. 50; Rick Bowers/Alamy, p. 51; Gerry Pearce/Science Source, p. 52; Danita Delimont/Alamy, p. 55; Byron Jorjorian/Alamy, p. 57; Tom McHugh/Science Source, p. 61; Author Photo Courtesy of Maaike Starkey

ISBN: Print 978-1-64739-042-6 | eBook 978-1-64739-043-3

RO

Printed in China

CONTENTS

MEET THE SNAKES (CONTINUED)

WELCOME, JUNIOR SCIENTIST!

I have been obsessed with snakes my whole life. What's not to love? Snakes are scaly and cold-blooded; they have fangs and rattles. These animals are amazing! As a child growing up in the city, I loved visiting the local zoo and kept pet snakes in my bedroom. As I grew older, I was excited to learn that there are jobs for people who want to spend their days working with snakes. I am now a wildlife biologist. From studying frogs in Central America to working with wildlife conservation groups to protect snakes around the world, I have been lucky to travel the globe and meet some of its most amazing reptiles. Guess what? You can too! If you love snakes, reading this book is a great way to start your future career as an explorer or scientist!

Burmese Python, page 25

WHAT IS A SNAKE?

Snakes come in all shapes and sizes. Even though they do not have limbs, these reptiles can slither, climb, swim, burrow, and glide. Snakes can be found on every continent except Antarctica, and some species even live in the ocean.

Snakes are very important animals for our world. As predators, snakes are a big part of the circle of life, but they can also be prey themselves. This relationship with other animals creates balance in the food web and helps keep **ecosystems** healthy. Snakes help us by eating harmful pests, and snake venom is even used to create new medicines that save human lives!

Yet, due to increased contact with humans, many snakes are **endangered**, and some **species** are even close to **extinction**.

The more we understand snakes, the better we can see how fascinating they are. Let's learn about them together!

Snake Families

Today, we know of about 3,800 species of snakes around the world, and scientists are still discovering new species. Because there are so many different types of snakes, scientists must work hard to name them all. To do this, they separate snakes that are similar to each other into groups. This way of classifying snakes and other groups of organisms is called **taxonomy**.

TAXONOMY

To understand taxonomy, let's use the neotropical sunbeam snake as an example.

The neotropical sunbeam snake is known by many other names: Mexican burrowing python, New World python, ground python, dwarf python, and burrowing boa. This unique snake is similar to both boas and pythons but is actually neither. It is the only species that belongs to the **family** Loxocemidae.

It can be very confusing for one snake to have so many different common names, so scientists give snakes and other organisms a two-word scientific name, also called a **Latin name**. That way, every scientist knows what snake they are talking about.

In this book, we will name each snake with one of its common names followed by its scientific name, which will always be in italics.

Here is the taxonomy of the neotropical sunbeam snake (*Loxocemus bicolor*):

This snake is an animal, so it is in the **kingdom** Animalia.

This snake has a backbone, so it is in the **phylum** Chordata.

This snake is a reptile, so it is in the **class** Reptilia.

All snakes belong to the **order** Squamata, which actually contains snakes *and* lizards. So they are also put into a **suborder** called Serpentes.

The neotropical sunbeam snake is the only member of the family Loxocemidae, and so its **genus** is *Loxocemus*.

The snake's pattern is dark on top and light on the bottom, so its species is *bicolor*.

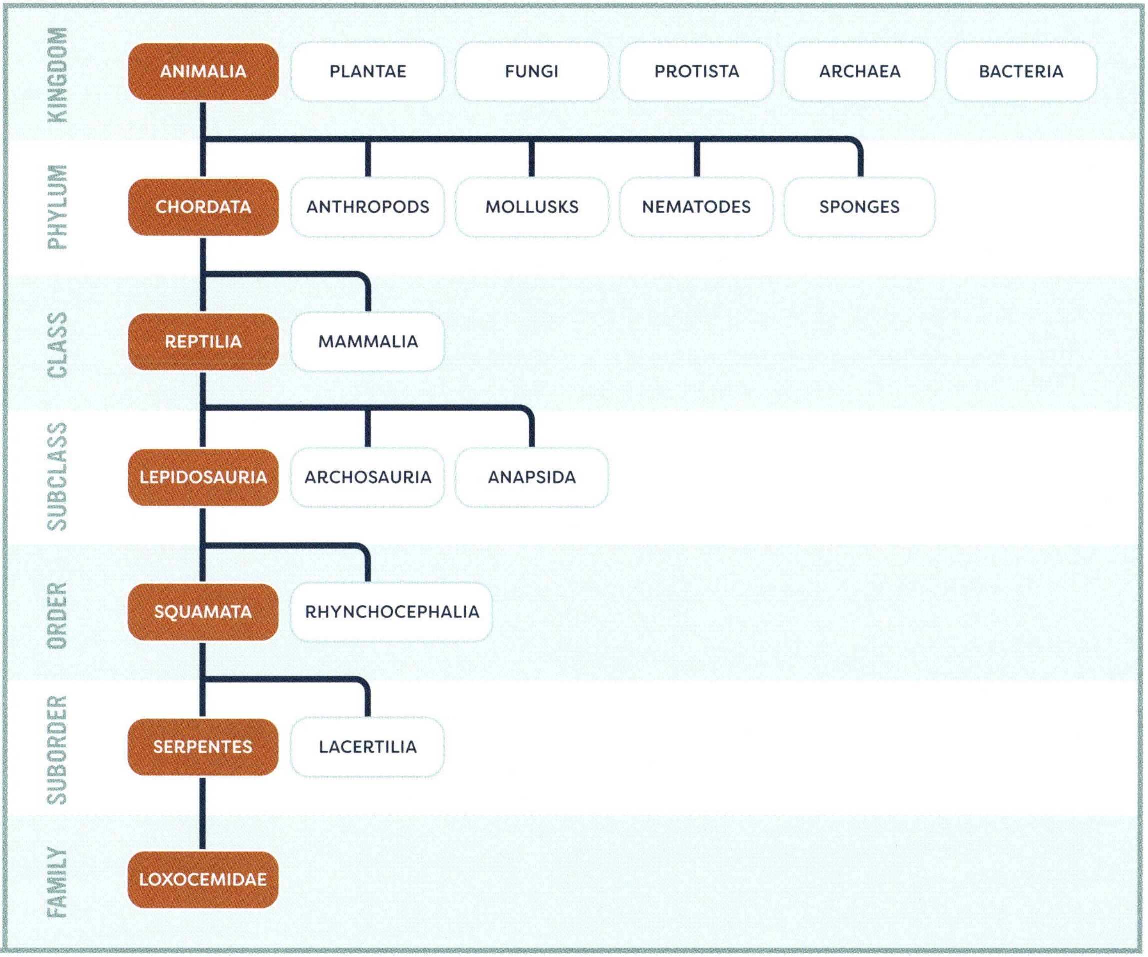

MYSTERIOUS SNAKES

What makes a snake mysterious? The following snake families are considered mysterious because scientists don't know very much about them. These groups of snakes are difficult to study because they are very good at staying hidden or because they live in remote parts of the world.

ANOMALEPIDIDAE

SAY IT! *Uh-NOM-uh-lih-PID-uh-dee*

Blindsnakes in the family Anomalepididae spend most of their life underground and can be found in Central and South America.

GERRHOPILIDAE

SAY IT! *JER-ho-PILL-uh-dee*

Blindsnakes in the family Gerrhopilidae can be found in South and Southeast Asia. Most species in this mysterious family have unique scales around their eyes that are divided in two, where most snakes have a single scale.

XENOTYPHLOPIDAE

SAY IT! *ZEE-no-TIE-flop-uh-dee*

Snakes in the family Xenotyphlopidae are from Madagascar and have a very large scale on their nose, which helps them dig underground.

ANILIIDAE

SAY IT! *AN-uh-LEE-uh-dee*

The brightly colored American pipe snake (*Anilius scytale*) is the only member of the family Aniliidae and is from South America.

BOLYERIIDAE

SAY IT! *Bo-LEE-uh-REE-uh-dee*

There are only two snakes in the family Bolyeriidae, and they are from the islands of Mauritius. Unfortunately, one species is now extinct, and the other is critically endangered.

XENOPHIDIIDAE

SAY IT! *ZEE-no-fuh-DEE-uh-dee*

The poorly known spinejaw snakes are in the family Xenophidiidae and live in Borneo and Malaysia. These snakes get their name from small spines along their upper jaw.

ANOMOCHILIDAE

SAY IT! *AN-uh-mo-KILL-uh-dee*

Snakes in the family Anomochilidae are **fossorial**, which means that they dig underground. These snakes can be found in the rain forests of Sumatra, Borneo, and Malaysia.

UROPELTIDAE

SAY IT! *YOOR-uh-PELL-tuh-dee*

Shieldtail snakes of the family Uropeltidae are burrowing snakes, which are **endemic** to India and Sri Lanka. Shieldtails get their name from their unique tails, which can be broad and flat or covered with spines.

LOXOCEMIDAE

SAY IT! *LOCK-suh-SEM-uh-dee*

The neotropical sunbeam snake (*Loxocemus bicolor*) is the only species in its family and is found in Mexico and Central America.

XENOPELTIDAE

SAY IT! *ZEE-noh-PELL-tuh-dee*

The sunbeam snake, whose scales shine like rainbows in sunlight, is one of only two members of its family Xenopeltidae, and it can be found in Southeast Asia.

PSEUDOXENODONTIDAE

SAY IT! *SUE-doh-ZEN-oh-DAWN-tuh-dee*

The snakes in the family Pseudoxenodontidae are medium-sized and live near forests or streams. They are found in South and Southeast Asia.

PAREIDAE

SAY IT! *Par-EE-uh-dee*

Snakes in family Pareidae eat mollusks, like mussels, snails, and slugs, and live throughout Southeast Asia.

XENODERMIDAE

SAY IT! *ZEE-no-DERM-uh-dee*

Snakes in the family Xenodermidae are secretive and nocturnal and can be found in Asia.

The Life of a Snake

Snakes start life as miniature versions of their parents. Even though baby snakes enter the world small, they are fully prepared to live on their own.

REPRODUCTION

The mating habits of snakes depend heavily on the climate. In colder parts of the world, snakes will usually mate after **brumation**, which is what we call hibernation for cold-blooded animals, in the spring. In warmer areas, mating occurs year-round.

BIRTH

Like other reptiles, most snake species lay eggs. Animals that lay eggs are called **oviparous**. The eggs must be kept warm, or incubated, until they hatch. Most female snakes leave their eggs shortly after laying them, but some snake species will stay with the eggs until they hatch.

Some snake species give birth to live young, which is called **viviparous**. Many mother snakes provide nutrients to their young before they are born, just like mammals (including humans) do.

Male snakes search for a female by following its scent trails. During mating, male and female snakes become entangled and join their tails. At the base of their tails is the **cloaca**, which protects and contains the reproductive organs that are on the inside of their bodies. The snakes do not stay together after mating.

In some snake species, like rattlesnakes, if two males encounter a female, they must fight for the right to mate. They will not kill each other but simply overpower the other with their bodies. It is quite dramatic!

LIFE CYCLE

Most species of snakes are considered adults after a few years. There is still a lot for scientists to learn about the life span of snakes. We think that some snakes, like the eastern worm snake (*Carphophis amoenus*), live for only one to two years. Other snakes live much longer, like timber rattlesnakes, which usually live 16 to 22 years in the wild. The oldest known timber rattlesnake was 50 years old!

Snake Anatomy

The ancestors of today's snakes once had legs, but through millions of years of evolution, snakes have perfected the art of being limbless. While you might think this would make their lives harder, a snake's unique anatomy helps it survive in the wild.

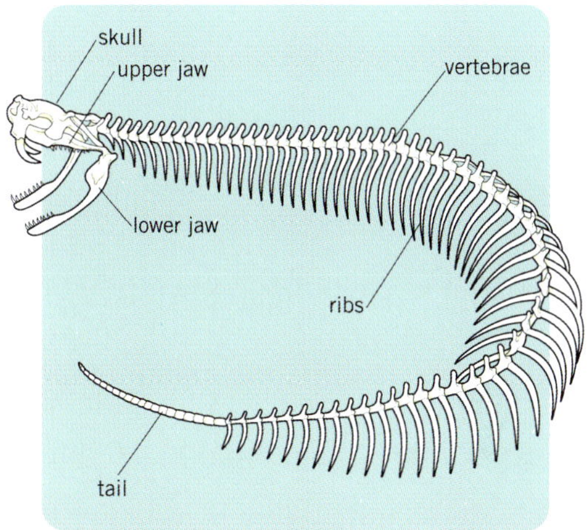

SKELETAL STRUCTURE

A snake's skeleton is very different from yours! A snake's skeleton is made up of a skull, a spinal column, and hundreds of ribs. Because snakes do not have arms and legs, they do not have shoulder or hip bones. However, some snakes, like boas and pythons, have what is called a vestigial pelvis: tiny leg bones inside their bodies left over from when snakes' ancestors had legs.

ANATOMY

Snakes' organs are long and narrow, just like their bodies. Snakes have lungs, but in most species, one lung is tiny and does not work. The first third of a snake's body contains its head, windpipe (trachea), gullet (esophagus), and heart. In the middle of the snake are the liver and stomach, followed by the gallbladder, spleen, and pancreas. Then coiled up are the intestines, trailed by the kidneys, reproductive organs, and colon.

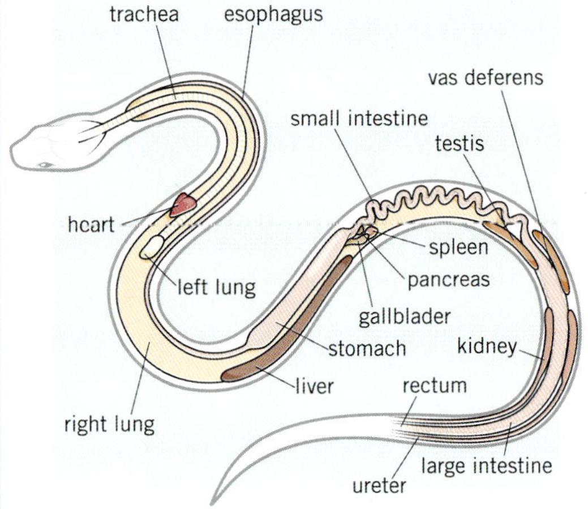

SKIN AND SCALES

Like other reptiles, snakes are covered in scales. Scales are made of **keratin**, just like your fingernails. The scales on top of the snake, or **dorsal scales**, are different from the scales on the bottom of the snake, the **ventral scales**. Dorsal scales act like armor and protect the snake from getting hurt. The ventral scales allow the snake to move. Snakes' scales are attached to each other by **interstitial skin**, which can be very hard to see. However, this stretchy skin can be seen in between the scales after the snake has eaten a meal.

Every species of snake has a different color or pattern on its skin, which is used to blend into its surroundings or to warn predators that it may be venomous.

Snakes grow throughout their whole life! This means that they need to shed their skin as they age in a process called **ecdysis**. Snakes shed their skin by rubbing their nose on rocks or bark, which causes the skin to split and roll off in one piece.

HEAD SHAPE

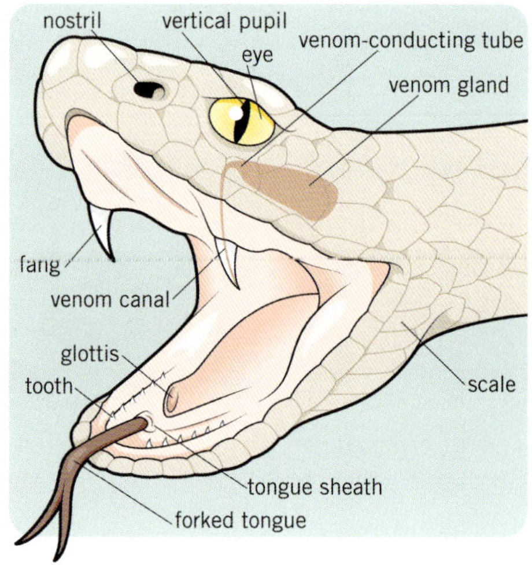

Snakes' unique heads allow them to use their incredible senses.

Snakes don't have eyelids. Instead, their eyes are protected with a see-through scale. Most nocturnal snakes, which are active at night, have slitted pupils like cats. Snakes with round pupils are usually diurnal, which means that they are active in the daytime.

Snakes do not have ears on the outside of their heads like humans. Instead, they have an internal ear on each side of their head, which allows them to hear low-frequency sounds.

The most interesting part of a snake's head is its forked tongue, which brings scents to the vomeronasal organ, also called the **Jacobson's organ**. This sensory organ allows snakes to "taste" the air with their tongue. As the snake flicks its tongue, scent particles are picked up, so the snake can follow or avoid scents in its environment.

Some snakes—like boas, pythons, and venomous pit vipers—have openings in their jaw that can "see" heat! These heat pits help the snake detect warm-bodied prey and even predators.

Snakes don't chew their food but only use their teeth to grasp prey. However, venomous snakes have hollowed-out teeth, called fangs, which deliver venom when these snakes bite their prey.

How Snakes Slither

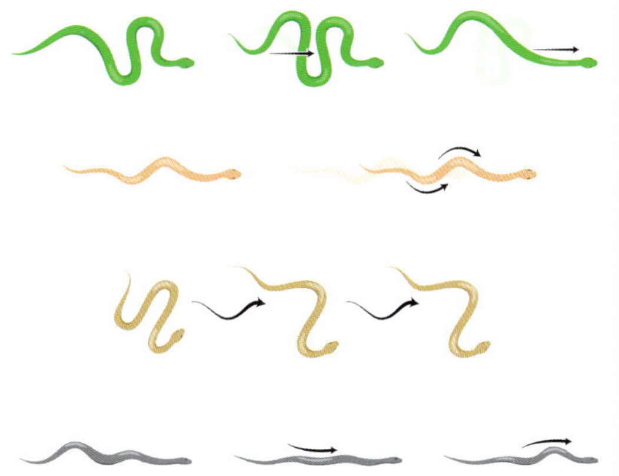

For millions of years, snakes have adapted so they can live in environments all around the world, which has caused them to move in some of the most surprising ways.

Most snakes move in a kind of movement called lateral undulation. The snake pushes its body from side to side to move forward. Snakes use lateral undulation both to move on the ground and for swimming.

Large snake species, like boas and pythons, can move in a straight line through rectilinear locomotion. These snakes propel themselves along by lifting their ventral scales slightly forward and then contracting their strong muscles to pull their body forward.

Snakes that burrow underground or climb trees can move using concertina locomotion, pulling their body into bends and then straightening out, which pushes them forward.

Sidewinding is used by many snakes that slither on slippery or loose surfaces, like sand in the desert. The motion is similar to lateral undulation, but the snake moves at an angle instead of straight, and parts of its body leave the ground, forming loops.

Snakes in the Wild

The wild is a dangerous, challenging place for any animal, and only the strongest survive. Snakes have evolved many remarkable natural behaviors that help them thrive in ecosystems around the world.

BODY TEMPERATURE

Like other reptiles, snakes are cold-blooded, or **ectothermic**, and rely on the temperature in their environment to regulate their body temperature. How do they do this? The sun! Diurnal snakes are active during the day and will bask in the sun's rays to warm their bodies. Snakes that are active at night and snakes that are active in between day and night will heat up on rocks and other structures that were warmed by the sun.

As the seasons change, snakes have adapted to dealing with the cold. Maybe you have heard of hibernating? Snakes do this, too, but scientists have a special word for hibernation of snakes and other reptiles: brumation. During brumation, snakes hide in deep burrows, hollowed-out trees, or caves—anywhere the temperature remains above freezing. A snake may use the same spot repeatedly year after year, decade after decade.

WHAT SHAPE SNAKE?

The body shape of a snake is connected with how often it moves and the environment in which it lives. Snakes that move a lot are usually slender. Thick-bodied snakes are normally less active.

The smallest snake known to science is the Barbados threadsnake (*Tetracheilostoma carlae*). It is only four inches long. This member of the family Leptotyphlopidae is found in the Caribbean, and it is small enough to coil on a U.S. quarter!

The reticulated python (*Malayopython reticulatus*) is the world's longest snake and has been recorded as reaching over 32 feet long. These powerful constrictors are found throughout Southeast Asia.

The world's heaviest snake is the green anaconda (*Eunectes murinus*). This large-bodied, aquatic snake lives in South America. Female green anacondas have been recorded to weigh as much as 550 pounds. That's more than twice the weight of a baby elephant!

DEFENSE

It may be hard to believe, but snakes have many predators. They also have many ways of protecting themselves.

Most snakes have excellent camouflage and blend into their surroundings to hide from predators. When detected by a potential predator, many snakes will flee. Some snake species are incredibly fast. The highly venomous black mamba (*Dendroaspis polylepis*) can slither up to 12 miles per hour!

If cornered by a predator, many snakes will hiss loudly and make their bodies look larger by puffing up with air. Cobras warn predators by stretching out their ribs to form a hood. Some snakes emit a stinky liquid from their cloaca, so that they will not be considered food. Some snakes, like hognose snakes, will even play dead. However, if attacked, snakes can deliver a painful bite.

Some harmless snake species mimic the behavior and color of venomous snakes to protect themselves. An example of this mimicry can be observed in nonvenomous milk snakes, as they look very similar to highly venomous coral snakes.

RATTLE AND SHAKE!

Native to North and South America, rattlesnakes have evolved a warning system to keep potential predators away. As the snake shakes its tail, it produces the characteristic "buzzzzzz." The rattlesnake's rattle is made of interlocking rings of keratin that make noise when they are shaken together. Each time the snake sheds its skin, it gets a new rattle segment. There is nothing else like it in nature.

DIET

Snakes are **carnivores**, which means they eat other animals. Some snakes eat many different things, and other snakes eat only one type of food. For example, egg-eating snakes eat only eggs. After a snake has eaten a meal, it must digest its food. Depending on the size of this food item, it may take a few days or even weeks to digest. Large pythons may only eat one large animal per year.

Some snakes use their body to overpower their prey! After they grab hold of the animal, they squeeze it until it dies, usually from suffocating. This process is called **constriction** and is commonly used by nonvenomous snake species.

Eastern Diamondback Rattlesnake, page 59

MEET THE SNAKES

Brahminy Blindsnake

Indotyphlops braminus

SAY IT! *IN-doe-TIE-flops bra-MIN-us*

The Brahminy blindsnake is a small, fossorial snake that burrows in fallen leaves and soil. Also called the "flower pot snake," this species likes gardens and plant nurseries. This snake has been accidentally moved around the world when people buy and sell potted plants! Because of this, it is the most widespread snake species in the world. The Brahminy blindsnake is parthenogenetic, which means that all snakes of this species are female and reproduce without males.

SNAKE STATS

COMMON NAME: Brahminy blindsnake	**COLOR:** Shiny silver, gray, or purple
FAMILY: Typhlopidae	**REPRODUCTION:** Oviparous
GENUS: *Indotyphlops*	**DIET:** The eggs, larvae, and pupae of ants and termites
SPECIES: *I. braminus*	**VENOMOUS?** Nonvenomous
DISTRIBUTION & HABITAT: Global	
SIZE: 2.5 to 6.5 inches	

Texas Blindsnake

Rena dulcis

SAY IT! *RAY-nah DULL-ciss*

After it rains in the Texas desert, you may notice earthworms crawling on the ground. Look closely. You could be seeing a Texas blindsnake. These little snakes are not completely blind, but their tiny eyes can only see light and dark. That's not a problem for these snakes because they live mostly underground. They sometimes surface after rain to look for food or when their habitat gets flooded.

SNAKE STATS

COMMON NAME: Texas blindsnake

FAMILY: Leptotyphlopidae

GENUS: *Rena*

SPECIES: *R. dulcis*

DISTRIBUTION & HABITAT: The deserts of southwestern United States and northern Mexico

SIZE: Up to 11 inches

COLOR: Pinkish-brown

REPRODUCTION: Oviparous

DIET: The eggs, larvae, and pupae of ants and termites

VENOMOUS? Nonvenomous

Cuban Dwarf Boa

Tropidophis melanurus

SAY IT! *TROH-pid-OH-fuss MEL-ah-NUR-uhs*

At three feet long, the Cuban dwarf boa is the largest member of the dwarf boa family. This snake is quite different from other boas, which is why scientists place it in its own family. To scare away predators, this small constrictor will squirt blood from its mouth and its nose, and around its eyes! Scientists do not fully understand this rare defensive behavior.

SNAKE STATS

COMMON NAME: Cuban dwarf boa

FAMILY: Tropidophiidae

GENUS: *Tropidophis*

SPECIES: *T. melanurus*

DISTRIBUTION & HABITAT: The forests of Cuba

SIZE: Up to three feet

COLOR: Dark brown, tan, or olive-green with greenish-brown blotches

REPRODUCTION: Viviparous

DIET: Small vertebrates, including lizards and amphibians

VENOMOUS? Nonvenomous

Elephant Trunk Snake

Acrochordus arafurae

SAY IT! *AK-ruh-KOR-duhs AH-ruh-FUH-ree*

The elephant trunk snake's name comes from its odd appearance. Its scales are small with rough ridges, and its skin is loose and baggy, making the snake look like an elephant's trunk. This strange skin protects the snake as it hunts for fish at the bottom of streams. Female elephant trunk snakes are much larger than males and can give birth to more than two dozen young at a time.

SNAKE STATS

COMMON NAMES: Elephant trunk snake, Javan file snake

FAMILY: Acrochordidae

GENUS: *Acrochordus*

SPECIES: *A. arafurae*

DISTRIBUTION & HABITAT: Coastal wetlands and streams in eastern Indonesia, Papua New Guinea, and northern Australia

SIZE: Five to eight feet

COLOR: Gray to light brown with a dark zigzag pattern

REPRODUCTION: Viviparous

DIET: Fish

VENOMOUS? Nonvenomous

Red-Tailed Pipe Snake

Cylindrophis ruffus

SAY IT! *Suh-LIN-druh-fiss ROOF-us*

The red-tailed pipe snake burrows in the moist ground of swamps and forests. It can also live happily in farming areas like rice fields. The red-tailed pipe snake is named for the round shape of its body. At the tip of its tail is a little patch of red. When threatened, the snake tucks its head inside its coils, flattens its thick tail, and displays the red as a warning to predators.

SNAKE STATS

COMMON NAME: Red-tailed pipe snake	**SIZE:** Three feet
FAMILY: Cylindrophiidae	**COLOR:** Iridescent dark brown body with lighter bands and a blunt, reddish tail
GENUS: *Cylindrophis*	**REPRODUCTION:** Viviparous
SPECIES: *C. ruffus*	**DIET:** Amphibians, fish, and other snakes
DISTRIBUTION & HABITAT: Wet, lowland habitats throughout Southeast Asia	**VENOMOUS?** Nonvenomous

Burmese Python

Python bivittatus

SAY IT! *PY-thon by-VIH-tah-tuhs*

Burmese pythons are one of the largest snake species in the wild. Because these pythons are calm and beautiful, they are popular pets. Some pet owners release their snakes into the wild, which has led to the Burmese python becoming an **invasive species** in southern Florida. These snakes naturally live in Asia, but there are fewer in the wild today, as people destroy their habitats and capture them for their skin.

SNAKE STATS

COMMON NAME: Burmese python

FAMILY: Pythonidae

GENUS: *Python*

SPECIES: *P. bivittatus*

DISTRIBUTION & HABITAT: Wetlands, grasslands, and forests of South and Southeast Asia

SIZE: Usually 6 to 16 feet in length, some recorded at more than 20 feet

COLOR: Tan to golden with brown or black blotches on the back and sides

REPRODUCTION: Viviparous

DIET: Mammals, birds, and reptiles

VENOMOUS? Nonvenomous

Reticulated Python

Malayopython reticulatus

SAY IT! *Mah-LAY-oh-PY-thon ruh-TICK-yoo-lah-tuhs*

The reticulated python is the longest snake in the world. The longest reticulated python ever found was 32 feet. When fully grown, this powerful constrictor eats wild pigs, small deer, and other large mammals. The reticulated python is the only snake known to prey on humans, but this does not happen often. This excellent swimmer can be found in wetlands and streams, but its population is declining as it is hunted for its beautiful skin and for use in traditional medicine.

SNAKE STATS

COMMON NAME: Reticulated python

FAMILY: Pythonidae

GENUS: *Malayopython*

SPECIES: *M. reticulatus*

DISTRIBUTION & HABITAT: Forests, grasslands, and wetlands in Southeast Asia

SIZE: Usually 6 to 25 feet

COLOR: Yellow, brown, and gray patches with small areas of white and a zigzag pattern

REPRODUCTION: Oviparous. Lays large clutches of eggs

DIET: Birds and mammals

VENOMOUS? Nonvenomous

Common Boa

Boa constrictor

SAY IT! *BOH-uh cun-STRICK-ter*

The common boa is a large, nonvenomous constrictor in the family Boidae. All across the Americas, this species includes many **subspecies**. Some subspecies are small and only live on islands in the Caribbean. Other, much larger subspecies thrive in the rain forests of South America and can be up to 13 feet long. The common boa is also called the red-tailed boa because it sometimes has deep red saddle-like patterns near the tail.

SNAKE STATS

COMMON NAME: Common boa

FAMILY: Boidae

GENUS: *Boa*

SPECIES: *B. constrictor*

DISTRIBUTION & HABITAT: Forests and near streams or rivers in southern North America, Central America, and South America

SIZE: 3 to 14 feet

COLOR: Brown, gray, or light tan with dark or reddish saddle-like patterns across the body

REPRODUCTION: Viviparous

DIET: Birds, reptiles, and mammals

VENOMOUS? Nonvenomous

Green Anaconda

Eunectes murinus

SAY IT! *Yoo-NECK-teez mew-REE-nuhs*

The green anaconda is the world's heaviest snake. While some anacondas can weigh more than 500 pounds, most are 60 to 150 pounds. Female anacondas are much larger than males, which is common in the family Boidae. Anacondas live most of their lives in the water, and their large size allows them to hunt for big prey, including caimans.

SNAKE STATS

COMMON NAME: Green anaconda

FAMILY: Boidae

GENUS: *Eunectes*

SPECIES: *E. murinus*

DISTRIBUTION & HABITAT: Wetlands and large bodies of water in northern and central South America

SIZE: 9 to 17 feet

COLOR: Olive-green with black blotches

REPRODUCTION: Viviparous

DIET: Birds, mammals, reptiles, amphibians, and fish

VENOMOUS? Nonvenomous

Emerald Tree Boa

Corallus caninus

SAY IT! *Koh-RAL-is kay-NINE-uhs*

Beautiful emerald tree boas are masters of camouflage. Their green skin helps these constrictors blend into their rain forest home as they ambush prey. These boas are nocturnal. To help them hunt at night, they have heat pits on their jaws, which allow them to "see" the body heat of their prey. When they are young, emerald tree boas are bright yellow or brick red. They become green as they grow older.

SNAKE STATS

COMMON NAME: Emerald tree boa	**SIZE:** Six feet
FAMILY: Boidae	**COLOR:** Light to dark green with yellow to white irregular banding
GENUS: *Corallus*	**REPRODUCTION:** Viviparous
SPECIES: *C. caninus*	**DIET:** Birds and mammals
DISTRIBUTION & HABITAT: Rain forest canopies of South America	**VENOMOUS?** Nonvenomous

Rubber Boa

Charina bottae

SAY IT! *Kuh-REE-nah BOTT-eye*

Unlike most boa species, the rubber boa likes cooler climates. They can be found under logs, leaves, and rocks as far north as Canada. This small, odd-looking snake gets its common name "rubber boa" because its brownish skin is often wrinkled with scales that are smooth and tiny, making the snake look like a piece of rubber. Rubber boas have short, blunt tails that are very similar in shape to their heads.

SNAKE STATS

COMMON NAME: Rubber boa

FAMILY: Boidae

GENUS: *Charina*

SPECIES: *C. bottae*

DISTRIBUTION & HABITAT: Grasslands and forests in the western United States and British Columbia, Canada

SIZE: Two to three feet

COLOR: Usually tan to dark brown, sometimes olive-green or orange

REPRODUCTION: Viviparous

DIET: Mammals

VENOMOUS? Nonvenomous

Eastern Indigo Snake

Drymarchon couperi

SAY IT! *DRIH-mar-kun COOP-er-eye*

The eastern indigo snake is the longest snake in the United States. These snakes hold their prey with incredibly strong jaws, sometimes even beating their prey on rocks or the ground. With this amazing strength, indigo snakes eat rattlesnakes and other venomous snake species. However, this tough snake is under threat of extinction because of human development.

SNAKE STATS

COMMON NAME: Eastern indigo snake

FAMILY: Colubridae

GENUS: *Drymarchon*

SPECIES: *D. couperi*

DISTRIBUTION & HABITAT: Longleaf pine forests, oak woodlands, and palm savannahs in the southeastern United States

SIZE: Up to nine feet

COLOR: Black to deep indigo with reddish coloration under the chin and neck

REPRODUCTION: Oviparous

DIET: Mammals, amphibians, birds, and other snakes

VENOMOUS? Nonvenomous

FAST SNAKES: RACERS, COACHWHIPS, AND WHIPSNAKES

In the family Colubridae, there is one group of snakes that is incredibly fast. The coachwhips, whipsnakes, and racers from the genus *Coluber* are diurnal snakes that are found in a variety of habitats throughout the Americas. These snakes have excellent vision and are often seen "periscoping," which means they lift their head and neck off the ground in order to better see their environment. Their good sight and quick movement are perfect for hunting one of their favorite meals: lizards. These nonvenomous constrictors can chase down their prey with lightning speed.

San Diego Gopher Snake

Pituophis catenifer annectens

SAY IT! *PIT-too-oh-fuss KAH-ten-uh-fur an-NECK-tens*

The San Diego gopher snake lives in grasslands, woodlands, and deserts in Southern California. It is often mistaken for a rattlesnake because of its defense behavior. When threatened, this snake puffs up its body with air and forms the shape of an S, a striking position. It also flattens its head so that it looks like the triangular head of a rattlesnake. The gopher snake then hisses loudly and shakes its tail, which buzzes to confuse predators!

SNAKE STATS

COMMON NAME: San Diego gopher snake

FAMILY: Colubridae

GENUS: *Pituophis*

SPECIES: *P. catenifer*; Subspecies: *P. c. annectens*

DISTRIBUTION & HABITAT: Grasslands, woodlands, and deserts in the western United States

SIZE: Three to six feet

COLOR: Yellow, tan, or light brown with large brown to black blotches across the back

REPRODUCTION: Oviparous

DIET: Gophers, rats, and other mammals

VENOMOUS? Nonvenomous

Rough Green Snake

Opheodrys aestivus

SAY IT! *Oh-FEE-oh-driss ess-TEE-vuss*

Rough green snakes are thin and harmless and are found in the eastern United States. These snakes are masters of camouflage. Their green coloration seems to make them disappear in plants. Their scales have ridges, which makes them look rough. While they live mostly in trees, they can often be found on the ground.

SNAKE STATS

COMMON NAME: Rough green snake

FAMILY: Colubridae

GENUS: *Opheodrys*

SPECIES: *O. aestivus*

DISTRIBUTION & HABITAT: Woodlands, grasslands, and meadows throughout the eastern United States

SIZE: Up to three feet

COLOR: Bright green with yellowish ventral scales

REPRODUCTION: Oviparous

DIET: Insects, spiders, and small amphibians

VENOMOUS? Nonvenomous

California Kingsnake

Lampropeltis californiae

SAY IT! *LAMP-roh-pell-tuhs CAL-ee-FORN-uh-ee*

Despite its name, the California kingsnake is not found only in California. These medium-sized snakes can be found in Arizona, Nevada, Utah, and even Oregon. Kingsnakes get their name because they love to eat other snakes, including rattlesnakes. California kingsnakes are constrictors and use their strong bodies to overpower their prey.

SNAKE STATS

COMMON NAME: California kingsnake

FAMILY: Colubridae

GENUS: *Lampropeltis*

SPECIES: *L. californiae*

DISTRIBUTION & HABITAT: Deserts, grasslands, and woodlands in the southwestern United States and northwestern Mexico

SIZE: Up to four feet

COLOR: Brown or black with yellow or white bands

REPRODUCTION: Oviparous

DIET: Mammals, birds, and reptiles, including other snakes

VENOMOUS? Nonvenomous

VENOMOUS SNAKES

Snake venom is a mixture of proteins, enzymes, and toxins that are used to immobilize and digest prey. Some snakes, like spitting cobras, use their venom for defense. Depending on what species they are, snakes have different types of venom.

Neurotoxic venom impacts the nervous system. The most important part of the nervous system is the brain. This venom works by blocking chemicals (neurotransmitters) sent between neurons in the brain. Cobras, sea snakes, and other snakes of the family Elapidae usually produce neurotoxic venom.

Hemotoxic venom prevents blood from clotting and causes organ and tissue damage. Rattlesnakes and other snakes of the family Viperidae produce hemotoxins.

Cytotoxic venom destroys cells. Cardiotoxins are cytotoxins that damage heart cells. Myotoxins damage muscle cells. Nephrotoxins damage kidney cells. Some venomous snakes, like Mojave rattlesnakes (*Crotalus scutulatus*), have a combination of cytotoxic venoms and may also produce hemotoxins or neurotoxins.

Boomslang

Dispholidus typus

SAY IT! *DISS-fuh-LEE-duss TY-puss*

The boomslang gets its name because it lives in trees. In Dutch and Afrikaans, *boom* means "tree" and *slang* means "snake." As adults, these snakes are green and brown to blend into the trees. They are gray when they hatch and change color as they grow older. Unlike other snakes in the family Colubridae, these snakes are highly venomous. They hunt chameleons, frogs, and other prey from the treetops. Boomslangs like to stay away from people, so it is rare for them to bite humans.

SNAKE STATS

COMMON NAME: Boomslang

FAMILY: Colubridae

GENUS: *Dispholidus*

SPECIES: *D. typus*

DISTRIBUTION & HABITAT: Forests in sub-Saharan Africa

SIZE: Up to six feet

COLOR: Males are light to dark green, sometimes with black coloration between their scales; females are mostly brown

REPRODUCTION: Oviparous

DIET: Birds, reptiles, amphibians, and occasionally mammals

VENOMOUS? Highly venomous

Mangrove Snake

Boiga dendrophila

SAY IT! *Boh-EYE-ga DEN-droh-FEE-luh*

The mangrove snake is a member of the genus *Boiga*, a group of snakes known as the cat-eyed snakes because of their slitted pupils that look similar to a cat's. These long, thin snakes are excellent climbers and are nocturnal hunters. When threatened, these snakes strike repeatedly, delivering a painful bite to ward off predators.

SNAKE STATS

COMMON NAMES: Mangrove snake, gold-ringed cat snake

FAMILY: Colubridae

GENUS: *Boiga*

SPECIES: *B. dendrophilia*

DISTRIBUTION & HABITAT: Forests and mangroves in Southeast Asia

SIZE: Up to eight feet

COLOR: Black or bluish with yellow or white bands

REPRODUCTION: Oviparous

DIET: Birds, reptiles, mammals, and amphibians

VENOMOUS? Mildly venomous

Western Hognose Snake

Heterodon nasicus

SAY IT! *HED-uh-roh-don nah-SEEK-us*

The western hognose snake is named for the upturned scale on the tip of its snout that makes it look like a pig. This adaptation helps the snake burrow in loose, sandy soils as it searches for its favorite prey: amphibians. When threatened, the western hognose snake is known for its dramatic defense behavior. It will puff up its body, hiss loudly, and, if all else fails, play dead.

SNAKE STATS

COMMON NAME: Western hognose snake

FAMILY: Dipsadidae

GENUS: *Heterodon*

SPECIES: *H. nasicus*

DISTRIBUTION & HABITAT: Grasslands and prairies near wetlands and streams in North America

SIZE: Up to two feet

COLOR: Brown to tan, with dark brown spots down the back

REPRODUCTION: Oviparous

DIET: Prefers frogs and toads; also eats reptiles and small mammals

VENOMOUS? Mildly venomous

Ring-Necked Snake

Diadophis punctatus

SAY IT! *DIE-ah-DOH-fuss punk-TAY-tuhs*

The ring-necked snake is nocturnal and secretive and lives under logs, rocks, and dead leaves or grasses. While mildly venomous, these snakes rarely bite and are considered harmless to humans. They are known for their interesting defense behavior, where they curl their tails and expose their brightly colored ventral scales. This bright coloration continues around the neck to form a collar, which is why we call these snakes "ring-necks."

SNAKE STATS

COMMON NAME: Ring-necked snake

FAMILY: Dipsadidae

GENUS: *Diadophis*

SPECIES: *D. punctatus*

DISTRIBUTION & HABITAT: Woodlands in southeastern Canada, the United States, and central Mexico

SIZE: Up to two feet

COLOR: Gray dorsal scales with bright orange, yellow, or red ventral scales

REPRODUCTION: Oviparous

DIET: Earthworms, slugs, salamanders, lizards, frogs, and some young snakes of other species

VENOMOUS? Mildly venomous

Cape File Snake

Limaformosa capensis

SAY IT! *LEE-mah-FOR-moh-sah cay-PEN-suhs*

The cape file snake is a unique-looking snake, with ridged scales that give it a rough appearance. This species is completely harmless to people and is even considered good luck in some places. This might be because the cape file snake eats other snakes! It hunts other snakes, including venomous species, at night. The cape file snake might be immune to the venoms of other snakes.

SNAKE STATS

COMMON NAME: Cape file snake

FAMILY: Lamprophiidae

GENUS: *Limaformosa*

SPECIES: *L. capensis*

DISTRIBUTION & HABITAT: Forests and savannahs in central to southern Africa

SIZE: Up to five feet

COLOR: Gray body with white ventral scales and a bright stripe down the center of the back

REPRODUCTION: Oviparous

DIET: Other snakes and small vertebrates

VENOMOUS? Nonvenomous

Brown House Snake

Boaedon fuliginosus

SAY IT! *Boh-EE-dun fuh-LEE-jin-OH-suss*

You probably guessed it, but the brown house snake gets its name for its brown color and because it can be found in or near houses. These small, nonvenomous snakes live in Africa and are often seen near humans because they are attracted to the rodents that live in people's homes.

SNAKE STATS

COMMON NAME: Brown house snake

FAMILY: Lamprophiidae

GENUS: *Boaedon*

SPECIES: *B. fuliginosus*

DISTRIBUTION & HABITAT: Near human settlements throughout Africa

SIZE: Two to four feet

COLOR: Reddish-brown to dark brown with a light stripe on each side of the head

REPRODUCTION: Oviparous

DIET: Small mammals

VENOMOUS? Nonvenomous

San Francisco Garter Snake

Thamnophis sirtalis tetrataenia

SAY IT! *THAM-nuh-FIS ser-TALL-is TEH-trah-TANE-ee-ah*

Maybe the most beautiful snake in North America, the San Francisco garter snake is famous for its blue and red colors. This species can only be found on the San Francisco Peninsula. Unfortunately, this snake is an endangered species because its nice colors make it a target of the illegal pet trade, and its habitat is threatened by the building of houses and businesses.

SNAKE STATS

COMMON NAME: San Francisco garter snake

FAMILY: Natricidae

GENUS: *Thamnophis*

SPECIES: *T. sirtalis*; Subspecies: *T. s. tetrataenia*

DISTRIBUTION & HABITAT: Grasslands and marshy wetlands on the San Francisco Peninsula

SIZE: Three feet

COLOR: Blue/turquoise body with black and red stripes

REPRODUCTION: Viviparous

DIET: Mostly amphibians, also small vertebrates and invertebrates

VENOMOUS? Mildly venomous, harmless to humans

Grass Snake

Natrix natrix

SAY IT! *NAY-tricks NAY-tricks*

A great swimmer, the grass snake loves to hunt frogs in marshes, bogs, and other aquatic environments. When threatened by predators, these snakes put up quite a show! They play dead and lie on their back with an open mouth, sometimes with their tongue sticking out. And if this performance wasn't convincing enough to deter predators, they will often release a foul-smelling liquid from their cloaca.

SNAKE STATS

COMMON NAME: Grass snake

FAMILY: Natricidae

GENUS: *Natrix*

SPECIES: *N. natrix*

DISTRIBUTION & HABITAT: Throughout mainland Europe and parts of the Middle East, central Asia, and northwestern Africa

SIZE: Three to four feet

COLOR: Green or brown with a yellow/orange collar behind the head

DIET: Amphibians, fishes, and invertebrates like earthworms

VENOMOUS? Nonvenomous

Western Green Mamba

Dendroaspis viridis

SAY IT! *Den-DROH-ahs-piz VEER-ih-diss*

The western green mamba is a beautiful green snake species in the family Elapidae. The green mamba lives in trees and uses its excellent camouflage to hide from predators. Like other members of its family, the western green mamba has a highly venomous bite, with neurotoxic venom. Bites to people are rare, as this species is shy. However, if cornered, the green mamba will defend itself, and bites are often fatal.

SNAKE STATS

COMMON NAME: Western green mamba

FAMILY: Elapidae

GENUS: *Dendroaspis*

SPECIES: *D. viridis*

DISTRIBUTION & HABITAT: Forests and woodlands of West Africa

SIZE: Up to eight feet

COLOR: Vibrant green to yellowish-green

REPRODUCTION: Oviparous

DIET: Rodents, birds, and reptiles

VENOMOUS? Highly venomous

King Cobra

Ophiophagus hannah

SAY IT! *Ah-FEE-ah-fuh-guss HAN-nuh*

At 18 feet long, the king cobra is the longest venomous snake species in the world. King cobras thrive in large forests throughout South and Southeast Asia. This species is the only snake to make its nest in fallen leaves, which it uses to keep its eggs warm and safe. The mother actively guards its nest from predators. King cobras are shy and prefer not to interact with humans, but because of the loss of their forest habitat, these snakes are under threat of extinction.

SNAKE STATS

COMMON NAME: King cobra

FAMILY: Elapidae

GENUS: *Ophiophagus*

SPECIES: *O. hannah*

DISTRIBUTION & HABITAT: South and Southeast Asia

SIZE: Up to 18 feet

COLOR: Gray to olive-green with black and white bands

REPRODUCTION: Oviparous

DIET: Snakes and occasionally monitor lizards

VENOMOUS? Highly venomous

VENOMOUS OR POISONOUS?

Did you know there is a difference between venom and poison? Both substances are toxins, but their toxic effects depend on how they are delivered into the body. Venom is harmful when it is injected, like from a bee's stinger. However, poison is only harmful when touched or eaten, like eating a poisonous mushroom. Most snakes are venomous because they inject venom through their fangs. However, there are a few types of snakes from eastern Asia, the keelbacks (genus *Rhabdophis*), that are both venomous and poisonous! While they are already naturally venomous, these snakes eat poisonous toads, which also makes them poisonous.

Monocled Cobra

Naja kaouthia

SAY IT! *NAH-juh kah-OO-thee-ah*

The venomous monocled cobra is named for the O-shaped pattern on its hood, which resembles an old-fashioned monocle. This species lives throughout South and Southeast Asia in wetlands, forests, farmlands, and even cities. These cobras quietly search for food during the evening when they are most active. But when threatened by a predator, they spread their hood, hiss, and strike. Some monocled cobras can even spit their venom!

SNAKE STATS

COMMON NAME: Monocled cobra

FAMILY: Elapidae

GENUS: *Naja*

SPECIES: *N. kaouthia*

DISTRIBUTION & HABITAT: Wetlands, forests, farmlands, and cities in South and Southeast Asia

SIZE: Up to eight feet

COLOR: Brown to dark gray, with occasional dark banding and characteristic O pattern on the hood

REPRODUCTION: Oviparous

DIET: Mammals, reptiles, amphibians, and fish

VENOMOUS? Highly venomous

Central American Coral Snake

Micrurus nigrocinctus

SAY IT! *My-KRER-uhs NY-grow-SINK-tuhs*

The Central American coral snake, with its black, red, and yellow bands, is highly venomous. Other snake species, like king and milk snakes (genus *Lampropeltis*), mimic these colored bands to scare predators away. This means that when you see a snake in the wild, it can be hard to know if it is venomous. Follow this rule: If it's a snake you see, watch from a safe distance and leave it be!

SNAKE STATS

COMMON NAME: Central American coral snake

FAMILY: Elapidae

GENUS: *Micrurus*

SPECIES: *M. nigrocinctus*

DISTRIBUTION & HABITAT: Southern Mexico, Central America, and Colombia

SIZE: Up to four feet

COLOR: Banded with black, red, and yellow

REPRODUCTION: Oviparous

DIET: Invertebrates, amphibians, and reptiles, including other snakes

VENOMOUS? Highly venomous

Inland Taipan

Oxyuranus microlepidotus

SAY IT! *Ox-EE-ur-an-us MY-crow-LEP-uh-doh-tuhs*

The inland taipan is a venomous snake species that only lives in Australia. Its venom is so powerful that one bite has enough venom to kill 100 people! This fast and deadly venom makes the inland taipan the most venomous snake in the world. Despite this, the inland taipan is a shy snake and doesn't like to bite. Bites to humans are incredibly rare.

SNAKE STATS

COMMON NAME: Inland taipan

FAMILY: Elapidae

GENUS: *Oxyuranus*

SPECIES: *O. microlepidotus*

DISTRIBUTION & HABITAT: Semi-arid regions in central-east Australia

SIZE: Up to eight feet

COLOR: Brownish-green to tan with darker diagonal bands, sides, and tails

REPRODUCTION: Oviparous

DIET: Mammals

VENOMOUS? Highly venomous

Yellow-Bellied Sea Snake

Hydrophis platurus

SAY IT! *HI-droh-fuss PLAT-uh-russ*

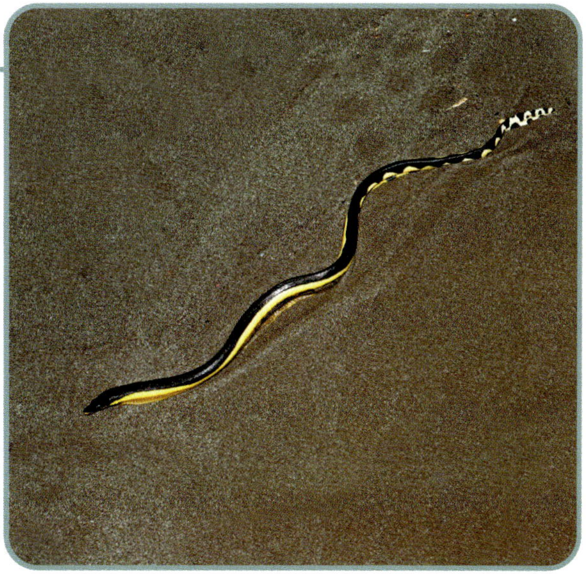

The yellow-bellied sea snake is a venomous snake that lives in tropical waters in the Indian and Pacific Oceans, so it can be found all around the world! Yellow-bellied sea snake venom is mostly neurotoxic, which helps slow the snakes' fast-moving fish prey. Like all other snakes, sea snakes need fresh water to drink. When it rains, the yellow-bellied sea snake drinks fresh water on the surface of the salty ocean water.

SNAKE STATS

COMMON NAME: Yellow-bellied sea snake

FAMILY: Elapidae

GENUS: *Hydrophis*

SPECIES: *H. platurus*

DISTRIBUTION & HABITAT: Indian and Pacific Oceans

SIZE: Up to four feet

COLOR: Black dorsal scales and bright yellow ventral scales. Some individuals are completely yellow.

REPRODUCTION: Viviparous

DIET: Fish

VENOMOUS? Highly venomous

Death Adder

Acanthophis antarcticus

SAY IT! *Uh-CAN-thuh-fuss ant-ARK-tih-cuss*

The death adder is highly venomous and is a master of camouflage! Its banded coloration makes it disappear among the dead leaves on the forest floor. Like many other vipers, the death adder is an ambush predator and waits for prey, sometimes for many days. When an animal passes by, the death adder strikes with incredible speed.

SNAKE STATS

COMMON NAME: Death adder

FAMILY: Elapidae

GENUS: *Acanthophis*

SPECIES: *A. antarcticus*

DISTRIBUTION & HABITAT: Forests and grasslands in Australia and Papua New Guinea

SIZE: Two to three feet

COLOR: Banded red, brown, and black

REPRODUCTION: Viviparous

DIET: Birds and mammals

VENOMOUS? Highly venomous

Tentacled Snake

Erpeton tentaculatum

SAY IT! *Er-PEH-ton TENT-ah-COO-lay-tum*

The tentacled snake is a truly unique animal and is the only member of its genus. This snake is completely aquatic and can stay underwater for up to 30 minutes at a time. It is the only snake species to have two "tentacles" on the front of its head that it uses to hunt fish. Scientists are still learning a lot about this mysterious snake.

SNAKE STATS

COMMON NAME: Tentacled snake

FAMILY: Homalopsidae

GENUS: *Erpeton*

SPECIES: *E. tentaculatum*

DISTRIBUTION & HABITAT: Murky streams or lakes in Southeast Asia

SIZE: Up to three feet

COLOR: Dark gray to tan with blotches or stripes

REPRODUCTION: Viviparous

DIET: Fish

VENOMOUS? Mildly venomous

White-Lipped Island Pit Viper

Trimeresurus insularis

SAY IT! *TRY-mer-ee-sir-us in-soo-LAIR-us*

In the bamboo forests on the island of Komodo, home to the famous Komodo dragons, there is another incredible animal: the white-lipped island pit viper. These small, nocturnal snakes are excellent hunters. Normally this species is bright green, but it can sometimes be yellow or blue. Blue is a rare color to find in nature, so it is exciting to know there is a bright blue snake that shares our world.

SNAKE STATS

COMMON NAME: White-lipped island pit viper

FAMILY: Viperidae

GENUS: *Trimeresurus*

SPECIES: *T. insularis*

DISTRIBUTION & HABITAT: Forests in Indonesia and East Timor

SIZE: Up to three feet

COLOR: Varying shades of green and blue

REPRODUCTION: Viviparous

DIET: Birds, mammals, reptiles, and amphibians

VENOMOUS? Highly venomous

Copperhead

Agkistrodon contortrix

SAY IT! *Ag-KISS-truh-don con-TOR-triks*

The copperhead is small and venomous and lives in the woodlands of North America. This snake species is known for its beautiful copper-colored head. Copperheads are ambush predators. Young copperheads even wiggle their tails to lure a lizard closer! But copperheads go hunting for one special type of prey: big, flying insects called cicadas. In the eastern United States, sometimes many cicadas hatch at once. These bugs are an easy meal for hungry copperheads.

SNAKE STATS

COMMON NAME: Copperhead	**SIZE:** Up to three and a half feet
FAMILY: Viperidae	**COLOR:** Light brown with tan to copper-pink crossbands
GENUS: *Agkistrodon*	**REPRODUCTION:** Viviparous
SPECIES: *A. contortrix*	**DIET:** Rodents, frogs, and insects
DISTRIBUTION & HABITAT: Forests in the U.S. Midwest and eastern states	**VENOMOUS?** Venomous

VENOM SAVES LIVES

While venomous snakes can be very dangerous, their venom is also used to save lives. Scientists discovered that they could cure the effects of a venomous snakebite with antivenom, which is produced using the snake's own venom! Antivenom is the only medicine that can cure a venomous snakebite. If someone is bitten by a snake, they must be rushed to a hospital immediately to receive lifesaving antivenom. Snake venoms are also used in drugs that help people. For example, copperhead (*Agkistrodon contortrix*) venom contains a protein called contortrostatin, which is being used to help people with breast cancer. Also, the neurotoxic venom of the black mamba (*Dendroaspis polylepis*) is being studied to treat brain injuries and brain diseases like Alzheimer's disease. Snakes save lives!

Cottonmouth

Agkistrodon piscivorus

SAY IT! *Ag-KISS-truh-don PIH-sih-VER-us*

The cottonmouth, native to the southeastern United States, is famous for its threat display. When cornered by a predator, the cottonmouth coils itself into a strike position, inflates its body, and opens its mouth. This display shows off not only its fangs but also the inside of its mouth, which is ivory-white. There are many exaggerated stories about cottonmouths being aggressive and chasing people. These stories are not true. Snakes are not aggressive but will defend themselves if necessary.

SNAKE STATS

COMMON NAMES: Cottonmouth, water moccasin

FAMILY: Viperidae

GENUS: *Agkistrodon*

SPECIES: *A. piscivorus*

DISTRIBUTION & HABITAT: Wetlands in the southeastern United States

SIZE: Three to five feet

COLOR: Light and dark brown crossbands. Some individuals are completely black or dark brown.

REPRODUCTION: Viviparous

DIET: Fish and amphibians

VENOMOUS? Venomous

Terciopelo

Bothrops asper

SAY IT! *BOH-throps AS-per*

This large, venomous snake is fast, irritable, and defensive. It has been given many names by communities across the Americas, including terciopelo, fer-de-lance, yellow jaw, and tommy goff. This snake usually lives near water, but has adapted to live near humans to hunt rodents in people's homes. This snake's defensive personality, highly venomous bite, and closeness to people make it the most dangerous snake in the Americas.

SNAKE STATS

COMMON NAME: Terciopelo

FAMILY: Viperidae

GENUS: *Bothrops*

SPECIES: *B. asper*

DISTRIBUTION & HABITAT: Forests of southern Mexico, Central America, and northern South America

SIZE: Up to six feet

COLOR: Tan, dark brown, and black crossbands with a distinctive yellow jaw

REPRODUCTION: Viviparous

DIET: Mammals, birds, amphibians, and reptiles

VENOMOUS? Highly venomous

Eastern Diamondback Rattlesnake

Crotalus adamanteus

SAY IT! *KROH-tuh-luss ah-DAM-ahn-TEE-us*

Meet the longest rattlesnake in the world, the eastern diamondback rattlesnake! This large, venomous snake is over seven feet long. It is also heavy, sometimes weighing over 30 pounds. These rattlesnakes are native to the southeastern United States. Unfortunately, habitat loss and being hunted by humans have made them less common.

SNAKE STATS

COMMON NAME: Eastern diamondback rattlesnake

FAMILY: Viperidae

GENUS: *Crotalus*

SPECIES: *C. adamanteus*

DISTRIBUTION & HABITAT: Forests and woodlands in the southeastern United States

SIZE: Up to seven feet

COLOR: Light brown with dark brown to black diamonds with lighter centers

REPRODUCTION: Viviparous

DIET: Birds, mammals, and reptiles

VENOMOUS? Highly venomous

Timber Rattlesnake

Crotalus horridus

SAY IT! *KROH-tuh-luss ho-ROD-us*

The timber rattlesnake is America's most famous pit viper. During the American Revolution, the timber rattlesnake was featured on a flag, with the words "Don't tread on me," as a sign of the United States' independence from Great Britain. This amazing snake species was respected for its standoffish nature. Unfortunately, today America's pit viper is under threat of extinction from habitat loss, infectious disease, and attacks by humans.

SNAKE STATS

COMMON NAME: Timber rattlesnake

FAMILY: Viperidae

GENUS: *Crotalus*

SPECIES: *C. horridus*

DISTRIBUTION & HABITAT: Forests throughout the eastern United States and in Ontario, Canada

SIZE: Up to six feet

COLOR: Yellowish-brown or grayish with dark brown or black crossbands

REPRODUCTION: Viviparous

DIET: Mammals, birds, amphibians, and reptiles

VENOMOUS? Highly venomous

Sidewinder

Crotalus cerastes

SAY IT! *KROH-tuh-luss suh-ROSS-teez*

The sidewinder is a venomous pit viper species that moves in a very interesting way. As this rattlesnake species is adapted to sandy, desert environments, it travels by sidewinding, which helps it avoid slipping as it moves across the sand. This species is nocturnal and will bury itself in the sand as it waits for prey to pass by. Young snakes will even entice hungry lizards close by using their tail as a lure!

SNAKE STATS

COMMON NAME: Sidewinder

FAMILY: Viperidae

GENUS: *Crotalus*

SPECIES: *C. cerastes*

DISTRIBUTION & HABITAT: Deserts in the southwestern United States and northwestern Mexico

SIZE: Up to two and a half feet

COLOR: Cream, yellow, gray, and light brown with darker-colored blotches

REPRODUCTION: Viviparous

DIET: Small reptiles and mammals

VENOMOUS? Highly venomous

King Cobra, page 46

MORE TO DISCOVER

RECOMMENDED WEBSITES

Save The Snakes,
SaveTheSnakes.org
Save The Snakes is an international nonprofit organization dedicated exclusively to snake conservation and human-snake conflict mitigation.

The Rattlesnake Conservancy,
SaveTheBuzztails.org
The Rattlesnake Conservancy was founded "... to advance the protection of rattlesnakes, and their habitat, through research and education."

IUCN Red List of Threatened Species,
IUCNRedList.org
The International Union for Conservation of Nature (IUCN) Red List of Threatened Species categorizes species based on their conservation status.

RECOMMENDED BOOKS

To read more about snakes, look for these books at your local library!

Awesome Snake Science! 40 Activities for Learning About Snakes by Cindy Blobaum

The Book of Snakes: A Life-Size Guide to Six Hundred Species from Around the World by Mark O'Shea

Katie of the Sonoran Desert: Based on a True Story by Kate Jackson and Linda M. Brewer (written in English and Spanish)

Snake: The Essential Visual Guide by Chris Mattison

Snakes in Question: The Smithsonian Answer Book by George R. Zug and Carl H. Ernst

GLOSSARY

BRUMATION (brew-MAY-shun): The hibernation-like state seen in reptiles during cold weather; garter snakes that live in Canada go into brumation during the winter.

CARNIVORE: An animal that eats other animals; as snakes are carnivores, they prey upon a variety of different animal species.

CLASS: The fourth-highest taxonomic rank; the class of snakes is Reptilia.

CLOACA (clo-AY-cah): An opening on an animal's body that is used for excretion and reproduction; birds, reptiles, and amphibians have cloacas.

CONSTRICTION: One way snakes use their bodies to overpower and kill their prey, usually by suffocation. Most snakes that use constriction are not venomous.

DORSAL SCALES: The scales on the top of the snake; dorsal scales protect the snake from its environment.

ECDYSIS (ECK-dy-siss): The process of shedding an outer layer of skin.

ECOSYSTEM (EE-co-siss-tem): The community in which animals, plants, and other organisms live. In an ecosystem, the plants, animals, food, water, shelter, and other features of the environment all affect each other.

ECTOTHERMIC (ECK-toe-THURM-ick): An ectothermic snake regulates its body temperature using outside forces; it might bask on a rock to warm up under the sun's rays.

ENDANGERED: An organism that is at serious risk of extinction; some snake populations are so low in number that the species is considered endangered.

ENDEMIC (in-DEM-ick): Organisms that can only be found in one region of the world; the inland taipan is endemic to Australia.

EXTINCTION: The dying-out of an organism so that there are no more left; some snake species that are endangered are at risk of extinction.

FAMILY: The sixth-highest taxonomic rank. There are about 25 families of snakes, including Viperidae, Elapidae, and Colubridae.

FOSSORIAL: Fossorial animals are adapted to dig and burrow. They live mostly underground.

GENUS (JEEN-us): The seventh-highest taxonomic rank, which defines a group of organisms that have strong similarities.

INTERSTITIAL SKIN: The skin between a snake's scales; after a snake has eaten, you can see the stretched interstitial skin.

INVASIVE SPECIES: An organism that is not native to an ecosystem and causes negative impacts to that ecosystem; the Burmese python is an example of a snake species that is also an invasive species in southern Florida, where it is causing harm to native wildlife.

JACOBSON'S ORGAN: An organ that detects scent molecules in the environment; a snake's Jacobson's organ helps it find its prey, avoid predators, and find mates. Also called the vomeronasal organ.

KERATIN (CARE-a-tin): The protein that is the structure for different parts of animals' bodies; examples of keratin include scales, horns, hair, and fingernails.

KINGDOM: The second-highest taxonomic rank; the kingdom of snakes is Animalia.

LATIN NAME: The two names, also called binomial or scientific name, that are made up of the genus and species of an organism; for example, the Latin name of the king cobra is *Ophiophagus hannah*.

ORDER: The fifth-highest taxonomic rank; the order of snakes is Squamata.

OVIPAROUS (OH-vip-er-us): Animals that lay eggs are oviparous.

PHYLUM: The third-highest taxonomic rank; the phylum of snakes is Chordata.

SPECIES: The taxonomic rank that defines a group of organisms based on similar traits, including the ability to reproduce with one another.

SUBORDER: The taxonomic rank that is between order and family.

SUBSPECIES: The taxonomic rank that defines a group of organisms below the species level; usually based on appearance and geographic region.

TAXONOMY: The branch of science that focuses on the classification of living things. Taxonomy helps scientists name animals and understand how animals are similar or different.

VENTRAL SCALES: The scales on the belly of the snake; ventral scales help the snake move.

VIVIPAROUS (VE-vip-er-us): Animals that give birth to live young are viviparous.

INDEX

ABOUT THE AUTHOR

MICHAEL G. STARKEY is a conservation biologist, ecological consultant, and public speaker working to educate and involve the public in wildlife conservation issues. From collaborating with communities to protect rare frogs in Ghana to tracking Yucatán black howler monkeys in Belize, Michael has worked with a wide diversity of wildlife from around the world. However, his passion has always been focused on snakes. He has worked on projects in California with San Francisco garter snakes, giant garter snakes, and northern Pacific rattlesnakes.

Michael is the founder and executive director of Save The Snakes, a nonprofit organization dedicated to snake conservation. He uses his knowledge, positive attitude, and enthusiasm for snake conservation to engage the public in protecting these beautiful animals. Michael gives educational presentations around the world to inform the public about the threats facing wildlife and to help nurture a society that respects and appreciates nature.